ISO 9001: 2015

Carlos H Hernández

ISO 9001:2015

Understanding ISO 9001:2015

First Edition in English, 2018

Serie: Management Systems

COPYRIGHT Carlos H Hernández

ISBN-13: 978-1984098535
ISBN-10: 1984098535

Contend

Introduction. 9
Structure. 9
    Conceptualization of the standard. 10
    4.   Context of the organization. 11
        4.1.   Understanding the organization and its context. 11
        4.2.   Understanding the needs and expectations of interested parties. 12
        4.3.   Determining the scope of the quality management system. 14
        4.4.   Quality management system and its processes. 14
    5.   Leadership. 19
        5.1.   Leadership and commitment. 19
        5.2.   Policy. 21
        5.3.   Organizational roles, responsibilities and authorities. 23
    6.   Planning. 24
        6.1.   Actions to address risks and opportunities. 24
        6.2.   Quality objectives and planning to achieve them. 25
        6.3.   Planning of changes. 27
    7.   Support. 28
        7.1.   Resources. 28
        7.2.   Competence. 32
        7.3.   Awareness. 32
        7.4.   Communication. 33
        7.5.   Documented information. 33
    8.   Operation. 35
        8.1.   Operational planning and control. 35
        8.2.   Requirements for products and services. 36
        8.3.   Design and development of products and services. 37
        8.4.   Control of externally provided processes, products and services. 41

- 8.5. Production and service provision. 42
- 8.6. Release and products and services. 45
- 8.7. Control of nonconforming outputs. 45
- 9. Performance evaluation. 46
  - 9.1. Monitoring, measurement, analysis and evaluation. 46
  - 9.2. Internal audit. 48
  - 9.3. Management review. 49
- 10. Improvement. 49
  - 10.1. General. 49
  - 10.2. Nonconformity and corrective action. 50
  - 10.3. Continual improvement. 52

QMS Control knob. 52

Brief implementation diagram of the QMS. 54

Glossary. 55

References. 57

Introduction.

The update of the standard ISO 9001:2008 to 2015 version, generated high expectations in experts and connoisseurs of quality management systems, even had those who dared to assert the same content, this caused uncertainty of what would be the scope of the 2015 version.

Many and important are the changes, starting from the number of clauses that go from 8 to 10, the analysis and approach based on risks that organizations commonly handled outside the system of management of quality, this to learn how the context of the Organization It affects positively or negatively the overall performance of the company. Another part of much relevance is that of the parties concerned, where is that senior management have very clear expectations of each to them taking into account or respond to them, noted as a relevant point that senior management takes one role more participatory throughout the system of quality management.
Concerning staff, acquires greater importance the knowledge of staff, that knowledge has to be both organizational and related to the post of labor and skills associated with the same. Finally all the approach is preventive concept, with the system definition and execution of these actions.

This book explains in a practical way what the organization can do to meet the requirements of the new standard ISO 9001:2015, explaining from clause 4 to 10.

Structure.

The new ISO 9001:2015 standard adopts the structure of high level, which already follow other rules of the ISO as a family: ISO 2700: information security, ISO 14001:2015 environmental management 2013, or the ISO 39001:2015 road safety. In addition, are expected to, as they will publish new updates, each time more ISO standards adopted this new structure of high-level or HSL (High Structure Level), which will greatly facilitate work integrative.

The new requirements of the structure are as follows:

- ➢ The risk-based thinking: risks and opportunities analysis goes through all the processes and regulatory requirements.
- ➢ Context of the Organization: it must have a knowledge of the internal and external context as well as the needs and expectations of interested parties, these should help drive the correct definition of the scope of the management system. It also

makes it possible to analyze and predict the critical factors (internal and external) that can affect the Organization's ability to achieve the desired results.
- ➤ Leadership: Senior management should show leadership and commitment to the implementation of the management system is integrated in the processes of strategic management of the organization.
- ➤ Planning: Allows the Organization realize the opportunities offered by the context of reference, analyze related risks and prevent negative impacts that may affect the achievement of the objectives.
- ➤ Documented information: every organization can choose the best ways to prepare and preserve documents related to its operations.
- ➤ Knowledge management: knowledge and people skills are elevated to the status of requirement, are considered a key element for achieving the objectives of the Organization and not to lose the accumulated knowledge of the organization.

Conceptualization of the standard.

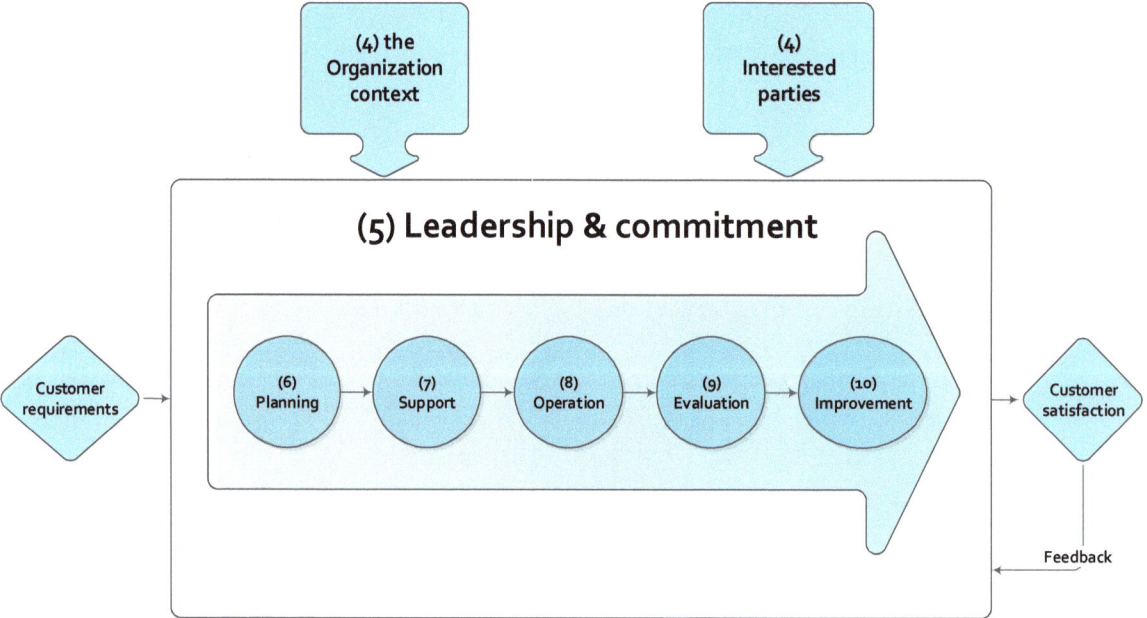

4. Context of the organization.
4.1. Understanding the organization and its context.

The Organization must clearly understand the internal and external factors that are relevant to the purpose of the Organization and its strategic direction that may affect the Organization positively or negatively. Context revisions must be at planned intervals and revised by the management review.

Sources of information for internal and external factors can come from different sources: public information, internal documents and meetings, publications, meetings with clients, etc.

The technique most used to understand the context of the organization is called SWOT analysis, which examines the strengths, opportunities, weaknesses and threats. It is commonly supplemented with the analysis PESTLA, this analysis helps in understanding the external factors that may have an impact on the organization. For the analysis of market competitive Michel Porter 5 forces analysis can be used.

Example of SWOT Matrix

Internal Factors	External Factors
Strengths • Leaders in the market. • High capacity for innovation. • Excellent distribution network. • Agreements with client-to-medium-term. • Excellent operational infrastructure. • 80% in market share.	Opportunities • Companies in the region are addressing local markets. • Signing of new trade agreements with countries outside the region. • Diversification of suppliers in the supply chain. • Geographical area with growing demand.
Weaknesses • Difficulty to find operators trained in new technologies. • Overall performance of the organization with negative trend. • Lack of training according to the reality of the Organization.	Threats • Forecasts of inflation due to increases in oil. • Difficulties in access to business credit. • Unstable country's political situation. • New regulations for the industry. • Entry of products imported with lower costs.

These internal and external factors should be helpful when implementing the corporate strategy of the Organization, normally strategies can be 4 categories: offensive, defensive, Adaptive and survival.

Also, it is very healthy at the time of this analysis involving the leaders of each process in order to not omit details that may affect the performance of the QMS.

This analysis should be documented and carried out on a regular basis according to what was planned by senior management.

4.2. Understanding the needs and expectations of interested parties.

Important to define who the interested parties are, whose impact may have in the Organization, which influence have on the QMS, so it should be considered when making the QMS planning.

Thus, it can be considered interested parties to the set of factors both internal and external that can have a positive or negative influence on the Organization.

The Organization should be considered in the interested parties the possible influence or impact on the performance of the Organization and decisions, the ability to create risks and opportunities, the influence that they have on the market.

Examples of interested parties:

Clients.
Beneficiary or end users.
Owners and shareholders of the company.
Bankers.
External suppliers.
Employees and other persons working on behalf of the Organization.
Legal and regulatory authorities (local, regional, state/provincial, national or international).
Unions of workers.
Social or community organizations.
Trade and professional associations.
Non-governmental organizations.
Neighbors activities.
Competitors.

The requirements of the interested parties linked to the QMS must be recognized, they can be summarized in an example table such as the following:

Relationship of the interested parties with the QMS

Interested party	Requirements for QMS	Relationship with the QMS
Clients	Commodity prices	Authorized price list
	Terms of delivery of products	List of customers packaging requirements
Bankers	Monthly payment of funding	Amortizations for project financing

Carry an assessment of how the party can affect our ability to meet the requirements with customers, legal, own and of the standard.

The customer's requirements: meet the expectations and the needs of our customers.
Legal requirements: it is a requirement that determines a regulatory body.
Own requirements: those who have to meet based on the operation of the organization.

Requirements: You must require by standard ISO 9001:2015.

To determine the importance of each of the interested parties, we can ask the following questions:

Is the interested party to paralyze operations capable?
Is it possible for the interested party to modify our process or our goods or services?
We have confidence in the interested party to work long-term with the success of the Organization?

Finally, the Organization must document, monitor and review the relevant requirements of the interested parties and reviewed during management review.

4.3. Determining the scope of the quality management system.

The scope of the QMS shall be based on the context of the Organization, the relevant requirements of the interested parties and products that are provided by the organization. This scope should clearly define the borders of the QMS whereas the infrastructure of the Organization, the different sites and activities, commercial and strategic policies, as well as the definition of the products and services.

This scope must be kept as documented information, you must include details of products and services covered, also the justification of any requirement that is considered to be not applicable.

The scope of the QMS must be in total consistency with the Vision, mission and values of the Organization.

4.4. Quality management system and its processes.

4.4.1. What is sought in this clause is that the organization determines the processes necessary for the QMS to be in accordance with the defined scope, all the main processes plus the support processes must be included. The level at which the processes need to be detailed may vary according to the context of the organization and risk-based thinking. The risk management proposed replaces the one that has been known until now as preventive actions.

It is important that as a first step should be a diagram in context, in which you can see the interrelationship of the main processes with interested parties.

A process is identified by the products that generates and measures based on the results it produces.

A convenient way to define a process is using the "SIPOC" model.

It is a model used to identify and clarify what is needed to create the product or service:

Suppliers: Entities that provide inputs to the process such as materials, information, and resources. Use the inputs of the process to identify suppliers.

Inputs: All materials, information and support (tangible or intangible) that are needed to support the process. A good way to decide whether it is worthwhile to add an entry to the process or is not, ask yourself "is this measurable input?" and "what if this entry is omitted?"

Process: These are necessary actions to convert inputs into outputs or activities. A way to check if something is a process is to see if it can be described as an action. Examples include measuring, flow, mix, cut and test, etc.

Outputs: The tangible results of a process. Each output of the process must be measured or measurable.

Customers: Persons or entities to which the output is created.

SIPOC conceptual scheme

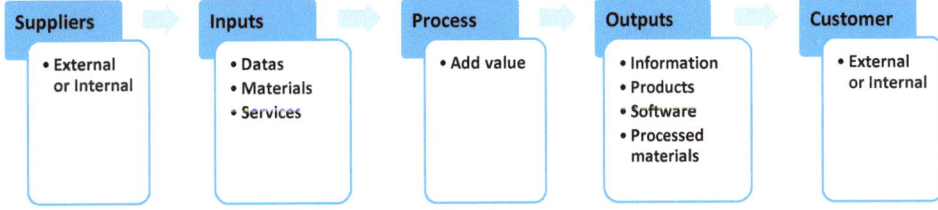

Example of context diagram - Flowchart of high-level

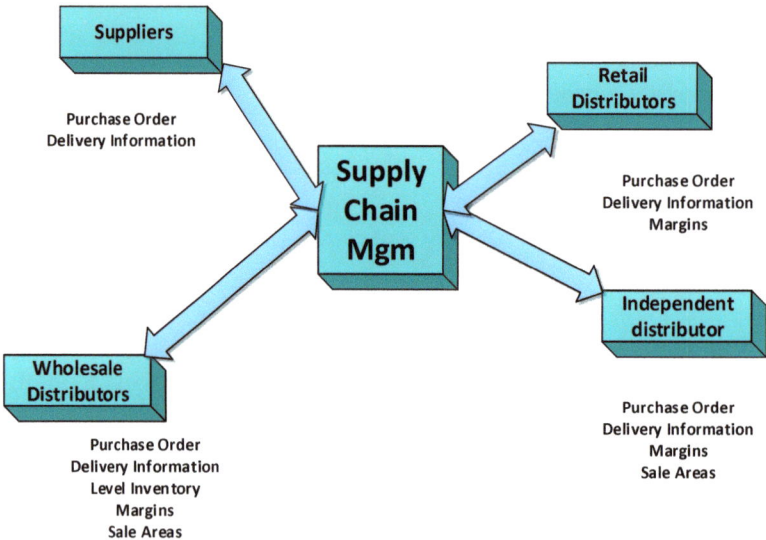

It is essential to start the layout of processes from the highest level in the Organization diagram and go spilling these levels until you reach a level of detail that leaves unclear how to operate each process within the organization.

It is vital that the organization is clear in the flow of important and determining processes in the operation of it. For this it is necessary to detail the flows:

Example of a flow of an industrial company

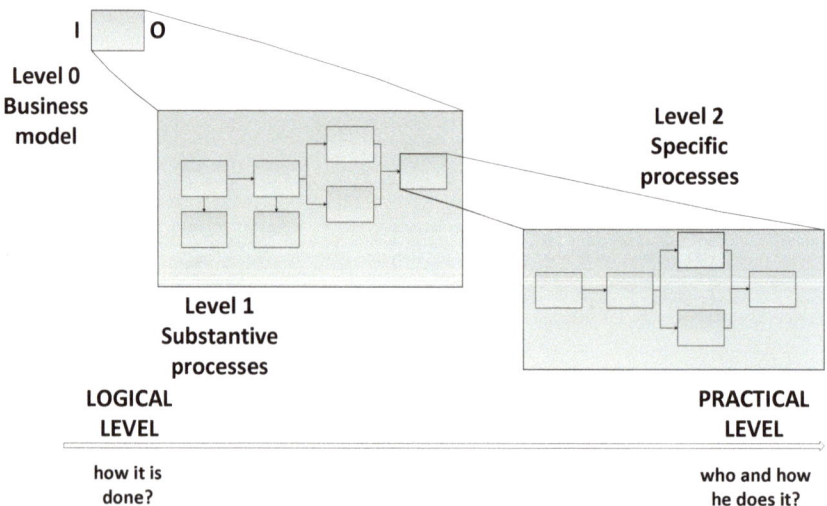

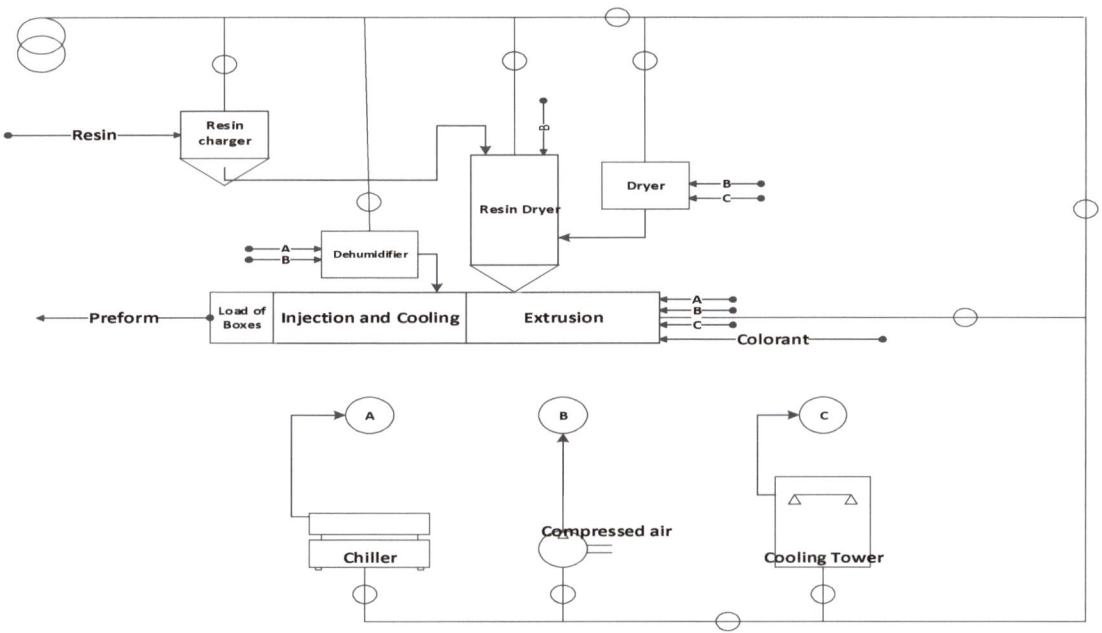

Turtle diagram example - Commonly used to manage and detail processes

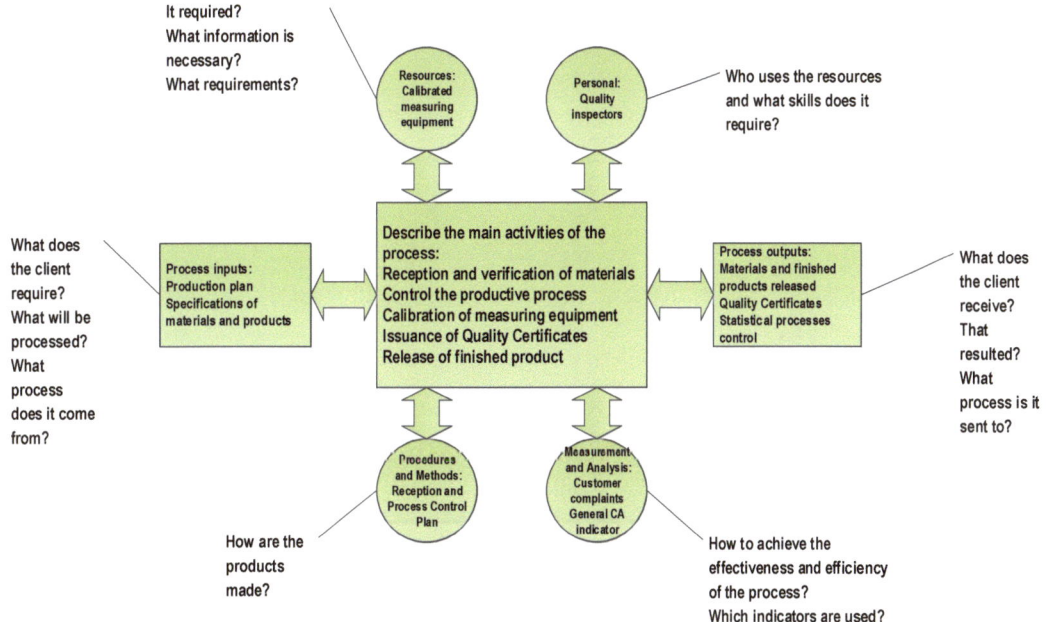

At this stage they must identify risks in each process, perform their analysis and evaluate it, to then define how it will be.

The identification must include all risks whether they are or not under the control of the organization. The objective is to generate a global list of events that could affect each element of the structure to which reference is made.

Once a global list of events has been identified, it is necessary to consider their possible causes and scenarios. There are many ways in which an event can be started. It is important that significant causes are not issued.

Identify management, technical systems and procedures to control risk and assess their strengths and weaknesses.

Also define the methodology to prioritize the risks found and finally define as they will be addressed each of the risks:

- Delete: Eliminate the cause (Not always possible)
- Transfer: That another part supports part of the risk (Think about what new risks this change causes)
- Reduce: Take measures to reduce the probability of occurrence and / or impact (It does not always imply additional financial costs, it can even save money)
- Assume: Accept the inherent risk or opportunities (But knowing it)

4.4.2. The organization must ensure that it has documented all the information it considers relevant for its proper functioning.

The leaders of each process should check the information used in its process and note that it is updated and is appropriate (which the process value). This information should be reviewed, regularly enhanced and keep up to date.

Finally each process should retain records demonstrating compliance and have confidence that the process is performing activities and obtaining the results as planned.

Documentation that should support each process varies according to the nature of the Organization, but this should be help to achieve the objectives set out in the process. Documented information can be: laws and external regulations, internal policies, procedures, work instructions, registers, manuals, information systems, diagrams of processes, specifications, minutes of meetings, Grill of indicators of performance, emails, etc.

Here process management is highlighted, which is one of the aspects in which ISO 9001: 2015 places special emphasis. In relation to this, the organization must specify the necessary processes for the Quality Management System and its application.

5. Leadership.

5.1. Leadership and commitment.

5.1.1. General.

It must ensure that senior management demonstrates leadership, commitment, interest, promotion, involvement in the QMS, must also communicate and monitor the performance of it.
The top management of an organization can include: CEO, Board of Directors, General Management, Executive Directors, Management Committee or simply the owner if it were small businesses.

Risk-based thinking should be promoted, ensuring the effective interaction of processes with a systematic design to achieve an effective flow of inputs and outputs and cooperation between them, this based on risks and opportunities.

Each process must have clearly defined the risks that may cause its process to be ineffective, that is at risk of not fulfilling expectations and causing harm to other related processes, as well as what it will do to avoid it and actions to take if they become a reality.

There are many methodologies to analyze risks, I personally recommend that you follow the methodology proposed by ISO 31000, then edit a guide to analyze risks.

The important thing of the selected methodology is that it identifies whether a risk is positive or negative, what is its cause, what the impacts are in the results, what is the probability or term of occurrence, thus this way it will be possible to elaborate a Risk and Opportunity Adaptation Plan.

Senior management has the power to delegate authority and provide all resources to the organization for the proper performance of the QMS, providing resources and verifying that they are always available, in order to ensure that each process is able to meet its objectives.

Effective and committed leadership can lead to a better understanding of the people in the organization and how they contribute to the achievement of results by the QMS.

It is important to remember the characteristics of a leader based on principles: He constantly learns, he is service oriented, they radiate positive energy, they believe in other people, they move in balance, they focus their life as a great adventure, they understand and practice synergy, and they practice the personal renewal, finally lead the improvement projects of the organization.

Scheme of an effective leadership

5.1.2. Customer focus.

Top management ensures that the improvement objectives of the organization are in accordance with the needs and expectations of customers. It measures customer satisfaction and acts on results, whether favorable or unfavorable. It is necessary that the organization receives feedback with this information, in this way it can plan improvements in the products and services. Analyze and study the expectations of customers, anticipating. Then the organization can design the products and plan the distribution or marketing.

Communicates and allows all staff to understand the needs and expectations of customers. It is important that each member of the company understands that depending on how they perform their work, the satisfaction of the clients will be affected positively or negatively.

Develops a systematic management of customer relationships. The relationships start from the commercial attention of first contact to the after-sales service.

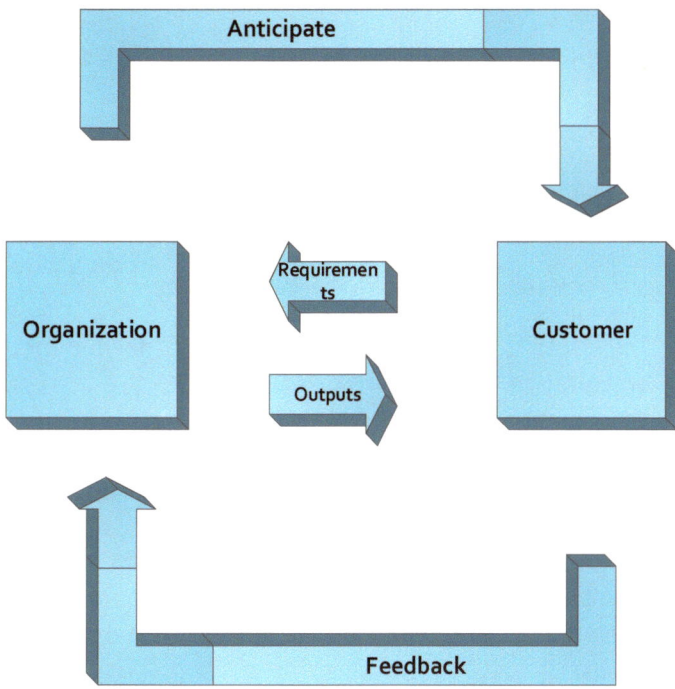

5.2. Policy.

The quality policy provides the intentions and directions given by Senior Management, this policy should be aligned with the strategic objectives and quality of the organization, in other words should support the purpose of the organization.

5.2.1. Developing the quality policy.

To make a good quality policy it is advisable to answer these simple questions that may be very useful:

What do we do?
What are our products or services?
Who is our ideal client?
What are the needs of the clients we can cover?
What differentiates us from our competition?

A good quality policy refers to the legal compliance applicable to the organization.

In order to establish the quality policy, the entries to consider may be the following:

- A clear understanding of the context of the organization, including the current performance of its management system and the needs and expectations of the main interested parties.
- The strategic direction of the organization, based on its mission, vision and values.
- The level and type of future improvements needed for the success of the organization.
- The degree of customer satisfaction.
- The resources necessary to obtain the expected results.
- The potential contributions of the interested parties.

The Quality Policy must be revised for its continuous adaptation and must provide a frame of reference to review and establish the periodic quality objectives.

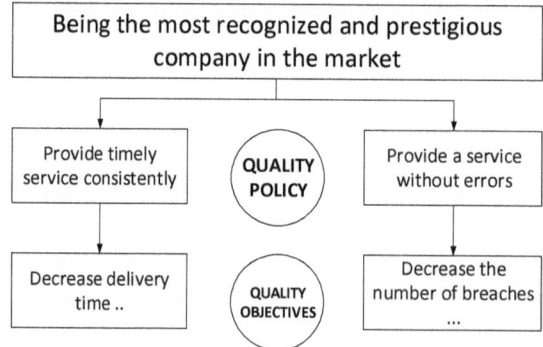

5.2.2. Communicating the quality policy.

The organization must ensure that the quality policy must be communicated to all staff, customers, suppliers and interested parties.
The communication must be made by means of signs through all the dependencies of the organization and in the web portal of the organization.
It must be ensured that it is understood and understood by all the personnel and mainly that the staff is clear about how it contributes so that said policy is effective in all the processes.

5.3. Organizational roles, responsibilities and authorities.

The top management of the organization assigns the relevant roles in relation to the QMS, in order to ensure the effectiveness and achieve the expected results. It is necessary to establish specific responsibilities and authority for the roles and ensure that the people in the organization understand their assignments through effective communication.

Roles and responsibilities must be defined in an organizational chart and a manual of functions and responsibilities, in this way senior management establishes the roles for the proper functioning of the QMS and avoid dissatisfied customers, lost business opportunities, confusion and bad internal climate. In addition, unnecessary waste of time, unsatisfied and unproductive workers.

To define roles and responsibilities there is a technique called RACI Matrix, which is a matrix of assignment of responsibilities (RACI by the initials of the types of responsibility) is generally used in project management to relate activities with resources (individuals or teams of job). In this way it is possible to ensure that each of the components of the scope is assigned to an individual or a team. There are also similar techniques: RASCI Matrix, RACI-VS Matrix, which are variations of RACI where additional roles are assigned.

Example of RACI Matrix

RACI Matrix	Person				
Activity	Aida	Andy	Paul	Fernand	Danny
Create Timeline	A	R	I	I	I
Get requirements	I	A	R	C	C
Submit change request	I	A	R	R	C
Develop exam plan	A	C	I	I	R

R=Responsible; A=Accountable; C=Consult; I=Inform

6. Planning.

6.1. Actions to address risks and opportunities.

Risk management is a vital activity in the planning of the QMS, the actions taken to address the risks and opportunities must be proportional to the potential impact on the compliance of products and services.

Options for dealing with risks may include: avoiding risks, taking risks to pursue an opportunity, eliminating the source of risk, changing the probability or consequences, sharing the risk or maintaining risks through informed decisions.

The opportunities can lead to the adoption of new practices, launch of new products, opening of new markets, contact with new clients, establishment of associations, use of new technologies and other desirable and viable possibilities to address the needs of the organization or those of your clients.

The risks are of an operational nature, that is, risks that are closely related to the processes, activities or operations carried out by the company. There is no talk of occupational risks or risks that occur in emergency situations.

Some methodology that can be used to manage the risks are:

- COSO
- FMEA

- IRM
- ISO 31000

Example of COSO structure

COSO Component	Level of identity	Process level
Control environment	Generally at entity level	Not at the process level
Risk assessment	High-level commercial risk assessment	Affirmations and account balance
Monitoring	Internal audit, self-evaluation	Monitoring incorporated in controls at the process level
Information and communications	Computer system, communication of roles and responsibility in the entity	Within a process as part of a control
Control activities	They exist mainly at the process level	They exist mainly at the process level

Example of FMEA Matrix

Component	Function	Potential failure mode	Potential failure effect	Severed	Potential cause of failure	Occurrence	Actuals prevention controls	Current detection controls	Detection	NPR	Responsible / Date	Recommended Actions	Action taken	Severed	Occurrence	Detection	NPR
100 W Focus	Transforms electrical energy into light to illuminate area	Burned	A focus does not illuminate	10	Poor quality focus	5	No	No	10	500	CH/ Mar 18	Select certified provider	Effectuated	1	10	1	10
		Insufficient	Illumination insufficient	8	Less powerful spotlight	5	No	Check list	2	80	AH/ Mar 18	Select certified provider	effectuated	8	2	1	16
				8	Focus does not meet specs	8	No	No	4	256	PH/ Mar 18	Select certified provider	effectuated	10	1	1	8

6.2. Quality objectives and planning to achieve them.

6.2.1. The establishment of quality objectives is one of the most important tasks during and after the implementation of a quality system. The objectives of quality must be established to the relevant functions, levels and processes of the organization, they must help to improve the performance of the organization. It is said that they must be SMART (Specific, Measurable, Achievable, Relevant, Time-bound). They should be updated as necessary.

It must be clear that it is a strategy, an objective and a goal.

Implementing a QMS is a strategy that aims to: increase customer satisfaction, reduce complaints, gain market share, achieve more efficient processes, etc.

Relation objectives and goals

Objective	Goal
Gain market share	- Lower manufacturing costs by 7%. - Increase customers by 10% in neighboring countries.
Decrease in transportation costs	- Replacing the truck fleet by 15% in the first year and 10% in the second year.

6.2.2. Normally the objectives and goals are related to an indicator, these should be controlled with a program that can have the following structure:

OBJECTIVE	DESCRIPTION	ACCOUNTABILITY	TERM	RESOURCES	GOAL AND FOLLOW UP	META INDICATOR
Gain market share	Establish guidelines in the organization to increase the presence of our products in the market	Head of Marketing: Renew exclusivity contracts with current and new customers Sales manager: Increase the frequency of weekly visits General Management: Create together with advertising agency Head of Logistics: Maintain the inventory with products according to the sales plan	March 2018	Humans: 2 hours per week in the restructuring of routes to increase frequency of visits Economic: According to the established budget of the company	Increase the participation in the first year by 10% Increase participation in the second year by 5% Monthly follow up	% Market share
Decrease in transportation costs	Add to each vehicle a fuel saver	Operations Manager: Plan with the purchasing area the acquisition of the fuel saver according	December 2018	Materials: Fuel Savers	3 changes of fuel savers per week	Cost per km traveled

OBJECTIVE	DESCRIPTION	ACCOUNTABILITY	TERM	RESOURCES	GOAL AND FOLLOW UP	META INDICATOR
		to the brand of the vehicle Workshop Manager: Schedule together with the sales area on the day the fuel saver addition is made			Monthly follow up	
	Replacement of trucks that have been operating for more than 10 years	General Management: Inform the truck replacement plan (Stages) Chief of Operations: Adaptation of the truck to the needs of the organization	December 2019	Humans: 1 hour per week of personal dedication	20% of the fleet subject to change each quarter Tracing: Quarterly	Cost per km travel of new trucks

6.3. Planning of changes.

The organization must determine changes in the QMS in order to adapt the changes to the business environment and also ensure that any proposed changes are planned, introduced and implemented in a controlled manner.

The purpose of change planning is to maintain the integrity of the QMS and the ability of the organization to continue providing conforming products and services during the change. The organization should consider actions that should reduce potential negative impacts due to the change.

The need for a change can be determined in different ways: management review, audit results, review of non-conformities, analysis of complaints, analysis of process performance, changes in the context, changes in the requirements of clients or parties interested.

All changes must be analyzed by the Management, ensuring the following:
- Why should it be changed?
- What will the change bring, what is expected from the changes (indicators and objectives)?
- What resources and needs are needed
- What risks can it involve?
- Viability study
- How will the change be planned

- What improvements will you provide to the organization?

It is very important the participation of the staff in the changes of the QMS, this participation must be encouraged and at the same time we must have a methodology to do it, the following steps can be followed: Request for change, Registration of change requests, Evaluate the requests for Change, Implement the change and Evaluate the effectiveness of the change.

Some examples of changes: New process plants, Changes in production lines, Changes in processes and methodologies, Changes in measurement equipment, New or changes in information systems, Changes in sub-contracted external processes, Changes in operational or managerial personnel , etc.

7. Support.
7.1. Resources.

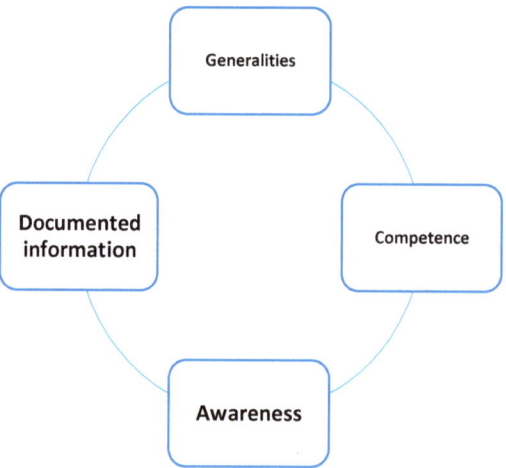

7.1.1. General.

To determine the resources that must be provided, the organization must consider the current capabilities of its internal resources and any budget constraints.
During the determination of resources, the organization can consider the cost-benefit analysis, using risk-based thinking.
When evaluating limitations of internal resources, it will be necessary to satisfy this demand through outsourced services, which requires monitoring to evaluate and control the performance of the service provider.

7.1.2. People.

The organization makes sure that it has the right personnel for the operation and control of its processes and the effectiveness of the QMS. The competences of the personnel must correspond to what is established in clause 5.3 Roles, responsibilities and authorities in the organization.

The burden of activities must not lose sight in jobs belonging to the QMS and the new skills required: activities operational, audits, inspections, testing, research claims.

The organization must decide if it will have its own or subcontracted personnel, in both cases the personnel must be trained and evaluated in the specific processes assigned to them.

The company that provides the subcontracted personnel must be clearly provided with the requirements that must be met and evaluated periodically.

7.1.3. Infrastructure.

Infrastructure achieves the most relevance when it directly influences the quality of the product, the organization must determine what infrastructure it needs, provide it or look for viable alternatives that support the effectiveness of the process and finally maintain it, means to keep it in perfect operating conditions. It is important to have a list of critical equipment and critical spare parts for them.

7.1.4. Environment for the operation of the processes.

All the daily activities have to be developed in an environment, this environment is known as a work environment, this involves in some way the organization and structure of the work, since the organization is embodied in the physical space, in this way the study of the work environment includes social, psychological and physical factors, because there is human interaction in the processes.

Factors to consider related to the work environment	Characteristics
Socials	Non-discriminatory, quiet environment, conflict-free, workplace harassment.
Psychological	Stress, exhaustion, care of emotions, excessive control, working hours and unsuitable working hours.

Factors to consider related to the work environment	Characteristics
Physics	Temperature, heat, humidity, lighting, air circulation, hygiene, noise, distribution of operations, ergonomic conditions.
Externals	Lifestyle outside of the work environment

Another term used today is work environment is toxic, is an environment where employees have to deal with stressful or unsatisfactory work conditions. Employees who work in a toxic environment have to deal with personality conflicts, intimidation, and lack of motivation or low quality work. People in toxic work environments may be less productive because they are stressed.

The organization must determine, provide and maintain the necessary environment for the ideal or basic operation for the proper development of the activities.

7.1.5. Monitoring and measurement resources.
    7.1.5.1.   General.

The organization must ensure that it provides the necessary resources to ensure that the measurement and follow-up are reliable and avoid problems in the products.

The types of measurement and monitoring equipment are according to the nature of the operation, you must have control of these resources so that they are always in good operating conditions and that there are personnel suitable for its maintenance and correct operation. The maintenance can be internal or external. It is recommended that there is a log where the history of the equipment is kept: general data and characteristics of the equipment, supplier and contact, date of acquisition, maintenance, updates, calibrations, verifications, date of withdrawal, etc.

Monitoring and measuring equipment can be used to record quantities, weights, heights, compression force, elongation strength, radial force, flows, temperatures, colors, etc.

7.1.5.2. Measurement traceability.

The monitoring and measurement equipment must give certainty that the data they are providing are reliable and therefore these equipment should be subject to a calibration and traceability program that includes the following:

- Contract that specifies the conditions of the service.
- The external company must have certifications that guarantee that it can carry out the maintenance and calibrations in a professional manner.
- Records of personnel training in the equipment assigned to them.
- Certified and traceable patterns.
- Schedule of verification of the equipment that specifies the frequency of revision depending on the use.
- Delivery of calibration certificates and identify the equipment according to its calibration and operational status.

If the organization has its own laboratory or personnel that executes these activities, it must comply with the required points to an external provider.

The organization must also make a risk analysis regarding the criticality of the monitoring and measurement equipment that are essential for the operation and therefore there must be an action plan in case a risk materializes.

7.1.6. Organizational knowledge.

The basis of the organization are the people, and specifically the knowledge that individuals or groups have about the products, quality, processes, customers, machinery, equipment, suppliers, raw materials, transportation, negotiations, information systems, legislation, formulas , recipes etc. to safeguard this knowledge the organization must be prepared and must make it available when necessary.

The key information must be documented, the experience of successes and failures must be shared, as well as all the knowledge that has been acquired in training, training, testing.

The organization must decide what the key knowledge is, how it will be maintained and how and to whom it will be shared.

7.2. Competence.

Labor competency is the ability to successfully respond to a complex demand or carry out an activity or task, according to performance criteria defined by the organization. The competences include the knowledge (Knowledge), attitudes (Knowing Be) and skills (Knowing How) of an individual. Thus, a person is competent when:

- Know how to mobilize personal resources (knowledge, skills, attitudes) and the environment (technology, organization, others) to respond to complex situations.
- Performs activities according to explicit success criteria and achieving the expected results.

Under this concept, the organization must determine, ensure and take action so that people have the skills required by the position they are performing, including subcontracted personnel, which may be based on education, training and experience. Competencies must be documented as self-evidence in the profile of the position and in the individual file of each person in the organization.

When an organization detects that its employees do not meet the required competencies, the organization must take actions to correct these shortcomings by taking actions such as: re-training, reassignment of functions, hiring / subcontracting new personnel. After the actions taken should measure the effectiveness of them.

7.3. Awareness.

Awareness is when a person reconsiders about an event or event, something that he did wrong and realizes that what he did or does is wrong then he decides not to do it or do it in the right way, which is to become aware. Awareness seeks to make the person aware of their responsibilities and the effects of the activities they carry out, whether they are beneficial or not.

The personnel that works in the organization must be aware of satisfying the needs of the clients, of the quality policy, of the quality objectives in which they are involved and of participating in the continuous improvement of the performance of the QMS.

The awareness in the activities developed must be constant and without exceptions. In order to achieve awareness among the staff, clear objectives must be met, effective communication with all the interested parties, constant meetings with the working groups and contributing to the continuous improvement of the organization.

7.4. Communication.

Each organization determines their internal and external communication needs, and looks for ways to make this communication effective.

An effective communication provides guidance and increases the satisfaction of the members of the organization, a clear and functional way is the implementation of a communications matrix that covers the most relevant points of the process or the organization as a whole. It is recommended that each process manages and manages its own communications matrix.

What to communicate	When to communicate	Who to communicate	How it communicates	Who communicates
Indicators report	Every 5th day of the month	To the different process leaders	Via email	Quality Manager
Non-compliant product report	At the end of the month	Operations management Finance management Plant manager	Via email	Head of Quality Assurance
Findings in employee payroll	When reviewing the payroll before posting	In charge of preparing payroll Head of HR	Written report	Auxiliary of HR

7.5. Documented information.
7.5.1. General.

The organization must maintain the documented information required by this norm, the regulation (of external origin) if there is a law that requires it and its own according to what is required by the QMS itself.

The documented information must be up-to-date and useful to achieve the effectiveness of the QMS. This can be elaborated physically or electronically.

7.5.2. Creating and updating.

Nowadays the documentation is created electronically, although this can be used electronically or digitally.

The organization defines the format it will use, by order and standardization it must always be respected, it must regularly include identification and description, logo of the organization, effective date, author, version, and number of pages. Depending on the type of organization, the documented information may be in more than one language.
A methodology must be defined that specifies how to update the documentation: when it will be done and who will do it.

7.5.3. Control of documented information.
- 7.5.3.1. The documented information must be available at the point of use (processes, departments) and protected from adulterations, improper use or damages that render it illegible. The level of control depends on the organization.

- 7.5.3.2. The organization must establish a system to control the distribution and access to documented information, it must say where it is stored and how much is its holding time.
Change control is also considered and it should be defined how the obsolete documentation will be handled.

8. Operation.
8.1. Operational planning and control.

The internal and subcontracted processes of the QMS need to be planned and controlled in order to achieve the quality objectives outlined, it must be ensured that the requirements are met and that action is taken if there are deviations in them, it must also be emphasized in controlling the risks identified that can generate changes in the activities of the processes.

General scheme of QMS control

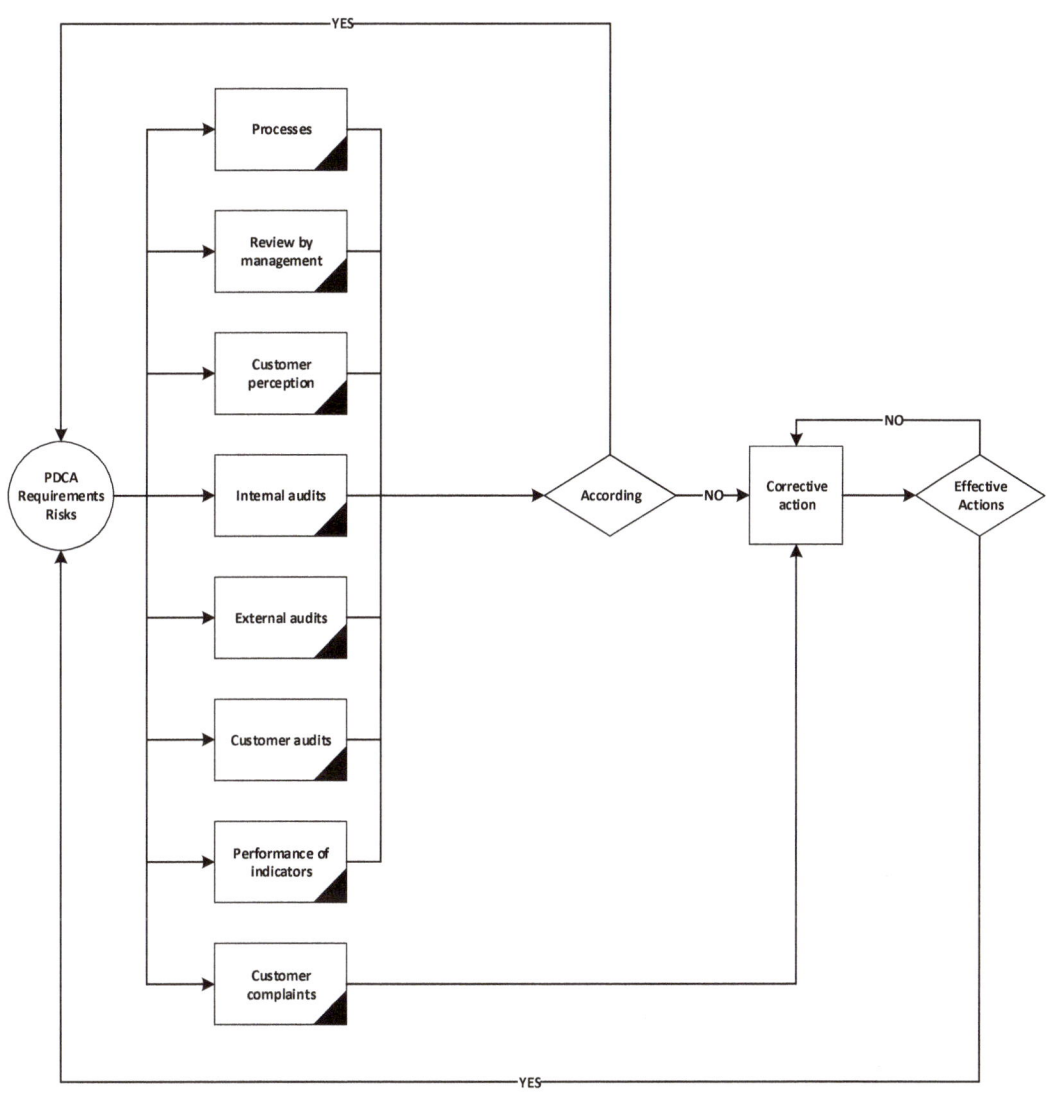

8.2. Requirements for products and services.

8.2.1. Customer communication.

The communication with the client must be stipulated in the communications matrix, it must be clear, precise, timely, proactive and must focus on determining the requirements of the products and services, obtaining the client's perception (concerns, doubts, comments, complaints, changes / modifications in requirements) and give confidence to the client that their requirements can be satisfied under control conditions including contingency states.

8.2.2. Determining the requirements to products and services.

At the time of obtaining the requirements of the client, these can be: Regulatory and legal requirements that must be met, requirements of the product and service, requirements requested by the client, internal requirements of the organization; these requirements should be used to plan how the client's request will be delivered. Internally, the organization must evaluate its resources and capacity.

It can be represented as:

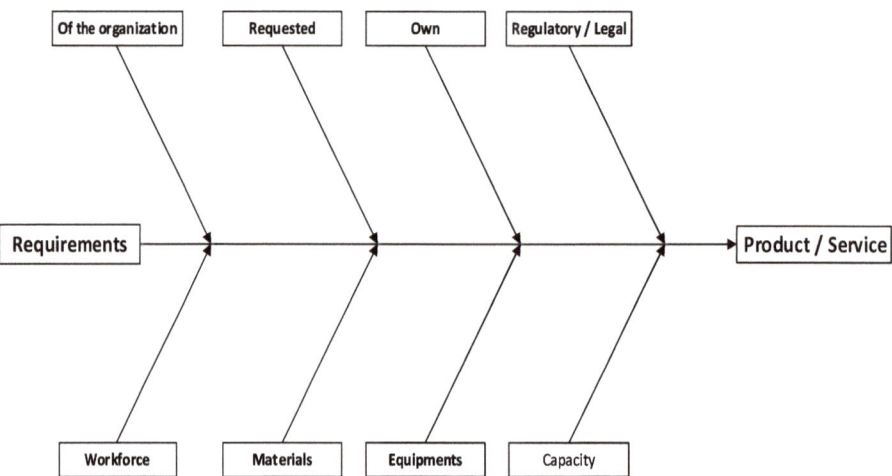

8.2.3. Review of requirements related to products and services.

8.2.3.1. The internal and external requirements must be reviewed and be sure that they can be met, every time the client requests a product or service, the requirements must be reviewed to verify that there is no difference with those previously established. This revision minimizes the risk of providing products that do not meet the established requirements.

8.2.3.2. When requirements are reviewed, the results of the review must be agreed and documented to demonstrate compliance with the client. It also applies to the incursion of new requirements.

8.2.4. Changes to requirements for products and services.

Modifications to the requirements must be made by authorized persons and communicated to the relevant parties. The documented requirements must be managed according to the document control methodology.

8.3. Design and development of products and services.

This clause has been restructured to achieve a more effective control over the design and development, placing great emphasis on the responsibilities of the personnel involved, inputs and outputs, controls, control of changes, authorization of change and necessary actions of the process to avoid adverse effects that may result in the final product.

The change control requires that the changes made to the products are documented, this is to have a complete traceability of the updates suffered by the products throughout their life cycle.

8.3.1. General.

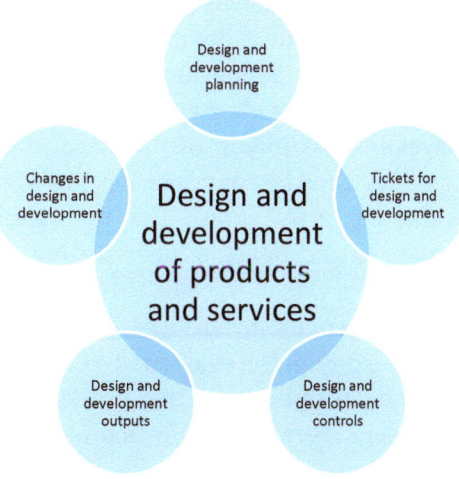

A design and development process must be established, implemented and maintained, for this the turtle diagram can be used.

For this process you must document your risk analysis to be able to manage them.

The organizations that have already established their Product Design and Development methodology can continue to use it once all the requirements of this standard have been met.

Examples of commonly used techniques:

Technique of the 7 steps

Brainstorming	The first step is to generate an idea for the product. Ask employees, especially those who deal with customers regularly, to get product ideas. Customer survey for feedback of existing products. Examine your industry to see if there are areas where useful products do not exist. Create an online survey for your customers or social media fans. List all the ideas for a new product.
Evaluate ideas	Make a list of product ideas and share it with those who make decisions in the company, such as the management team. Discuss the pros and cons of each idea and narrow the list down to just a handful of the best ideas, based on their potential to generate revenue, as well as the time and resources they have to actually create the products.
Market evaluation	Find feedback from customers, employees and partners on what idea is more attractive. Ask your customers for feedback via email or phone calls. Send an email to partners and employees, and ask which of the products looks more useful or valuable. Reduce the list to just one or two product ideas.
Analysis	Analyze the product idea that is in a business perspective. It determines how much, whatever it is, competition exists for similar products. Determine product demand and estimate all costs associated with the product, such as development costs and operating costs, to help determine the profit margin.
Prototype and marketing	Develop a prototype of the product, then share it with some good customers and key partners. Ask them to try it and provide feedback. The marketing team should use that information to develop marketing messages and develop ideas for marketing campaigns, such as email campaigns, websites, billboards or posters. Base marketing messages on the most common positive comments or reactions of customers and partners during the evaluation of the prototype.
Market test	Make adjustments to the prototype or develop a new version, if necessary. Develop additional prototypes for market tests. Make a small

	version of the product in selected areas. See if the product sells well and assess why sales are high or low. Evaluate the price and effectiveness of marketing messages. A small release helps determine what needs to be done before an official release.
Preparation for the launch	The production of the first round of the product launch begins. Evaluate the quantity of products to be produced based on your market analysis and product demand. Advertise and talk with the product distributors about the product acquisition, if the product will be sold in stores.

Also in this area there are other strategies that seek growth where the business goal is to introduce new products in existing markets. This strategy may require the development of new capabilities and it is necessary that the business produce new products or modify the current ones to satisfy needs not covered by the current market.

The processes used in this strategy are research and development, product policy and segmentation analysis.

8.3.2. Design and development planning.

The process must be planned using my experience following the turtle diagram methodology, which is represented below:

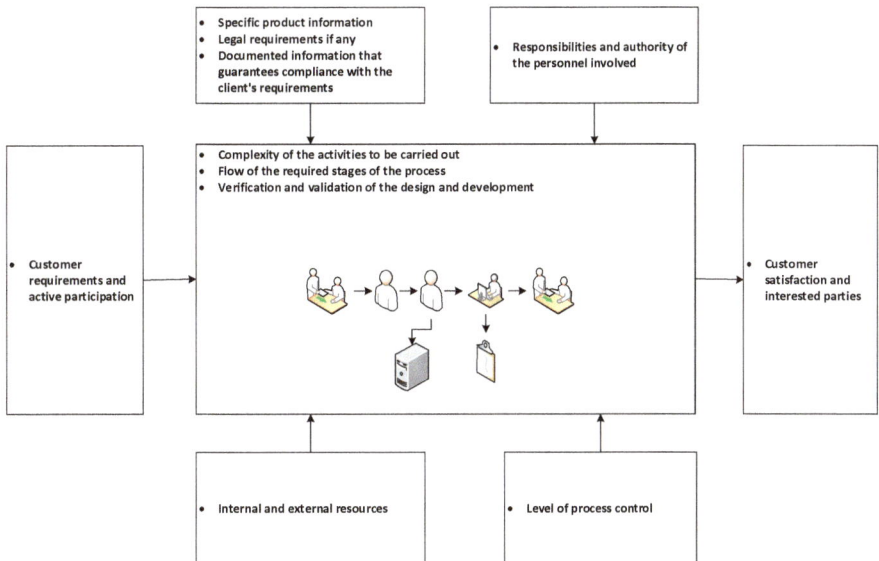

8.3.3. Design and development inputs.

The clearly defined requirements must be established (These must be documented) for all products involved in the process, considering the following: Legal requirements, Good operating practices, Operational requirements, Analysis of possible failures.

8.3.4. Design and development controls.

The organization must apply control at all stages of the process and can summarize it in a design control table:

Design stage	Specification / attribute	Control limit	Measurement equipment	Samples to be evaluated		Instructive	Control record	Check	Verify	Validate
				Size	Frequency					
Stage 1	Thickness of the material	0.5 ± 0.05 mm	Digital gauge	10	Every 2 hours	I-010	F-002	Designer Jr.	Designer Jr.	Design Engineer
Stage 2	Weight of the bar	5 ± 0.25 gr	Precision scale	5	Every 30 minutes	I-011	F-001	Designer Jr.	Designer Jr.	Design Engineer

The activities of revision, verification and validation must be carried out by different personnel.

8.3.5. Design and development outputs.

You must ensure that the outputs: Comply with the requirements of the established entries, are appropriate for the following processes, include the monitoring and measurement procedures, as well as the validation criteria of the product or service that requires it, specify the characteristics of the products or services that are essential, for the intended purpose, and suitable, so that they can be used safely and appropriately.

You should keep documented information about the outputs of the design and development process.

8.3.6. Design and development changes.

You will have to identify, review and control the changes that have been made in the design and development of the products and services, or later to the extent necessary to ensure that there is no adverse impact on compliance with the requirements. There must be traceability of all the changes that have been made and keep documented information to ensure that the change has been authorized and actions have been taken to prevent adverse impacts.

8.4. Control of externally provided processes, products and services.

8.4.1. General.

When the organization decides that certain processes, products, materials must be supplied externally, control over the suppliers must be implemented in order to guarantee compliance with the requirements established for these provisions, in other words, the organization is responsible for compliance with the established requirements.

External providers must be subject to a program where they are evaluated, selected, monitored and re-evaluated at established periods to verify that they are providing the service as established, which leads to the existence of documented agreements between both parties.

External suppliers can be evaluated through audits to suppliers, in order to know how they develop their processes and if they have the ability to meet our requirements, today this process is known as supplier development, where the purpose is for the supplier to accompany to the organization in continuous improvement.

The results of these evaluations should be sent to the providers as well as the opportunities for improvement if they have them and the records generated from this process must be documented.

8.4.2. Type and extent of control.

The organization must ensure that processes, products and services are provided externally and do not negatively impact the ability to deliver products and services fulfilling all requirements.

The organization has to make sure that all processes that are externally supplied are in control of the QMS, define the controls that are applied to an external provider and those that are applied to the products and services provided and the efficiency of the controls are applied by an external provider.

8.4.3. Information for external providers.

The organization has to ensure the requirements are adequate to communicate it to the necessary provider to: know the processes, products and services it provides, the approval of Products and services, methods, equipment and processes, releases products and services, competition, includes the required qualification of the persons, the interaction of the external supplier with the company, the control and monitoring of the performance of the external supplier to be applied by the company, all the verification activities that the company intends to carry out in the supplier's facilities external.

The control that must be carried out on the suppliers depends on: all the risks that are detected and the impacts that it generates, the extent that the supplier has control over its process outside its organization, the control capacity and the capacity to guarantee the efficiency of them.

8.5. Production and service provision.

8.5.1. Control of production and service provision.

This requirement aims to ensure that the production and operations activities are planned and then carried out in a way to ensure control. There are many different ways to achieve control and methods can include controlled processes, procedures, plans, specifications of materials and products, work instructions, quality plans, good operational practices at work and acceptance criteria in the processes.

To control the process, the organization correctly determines the total cycle of the product and service, from the beginning defining requirements to the use of the product and service, this includes the guarantees of the product. It should also show the risks in each stage.

The life cycle must be documented and each stage must show its characteristics, requirements and applicable controls.

The documented information used should become a standard and must include the following points:

Characteristics of products and services to be provided:	Material and product specifications must be available throughout their production cycle, this includes storage and handling conditions. The work instructions of the equipment to be used.
Resources to use:	Equipment to be used in good operating condition and with current calibrations.
Monitoring and measurement activities:	A correctly defined quality plan that indicates when, who, when, how to monitor each process control point.

Infrastructure:	All conditions of required infrastructure, industrial floors, temperature, lighting, ventilation, material flows, design of facilities, jobs.
Personal:	Number of people required by the operation and with the proven competences to be able to carry out the assigned activities.
Planned results:	Make sure that all processes comply with your established plan. Monitor the performance of the product and service in the client, have contingency plans in case something goes differently than planned.
Prevention:	Training to staff, personnel with non-excessive work hours to avoid exhaustion, avoid distractors, verification inspections, automated inspections by cameras and sensors.
Liberation:	Activities of final liberation of the product and service have to be detailed and making reference of the methods used, example Military Table or some other statistician.

A control system control system greatly prevents product and non-conforming services from reaching the customer.

8.5.2. Identification and traceability.

The organization must define what will be the methodology to identify the outputs of each stage of the process, these outputs must have unique identification and show their current status of availability.

The identification must be able to help traceability of the product and service: what materials were used, what equipment was developed, who were the operators, what date and time, who reviewed / authorized / released, product in good condition or not, etc.

This identification must help in case some product withdrawal will be necessary.

It is recommended that product traceability exercises be done to validate the effectiveness of the identification.

The customer must be shown the expiration date of the product.

8.5.3. Property belonging to customers or external providers.

The organization has to protect the client's property, take care that its use is strictly controlled, many times they are in charge of unique and patented materials, ingredients differentiated from the competition, promotional products, key financial data, and confidential customer data.
The client trusts that his business secrets are in good hands.

8.5.4. Preservation.

The preservation methods must be defined depending on the products and services so that they do not affect the client's requirements, important to document and disclose them with all the personnel involved.

The preservation must include materials, intermediate products, completions and services to third parties (example: internet, telephone service, etc.) throughout its cycle since they arrive at the organization, verified by means of a reception checklist until the delivery of the product and customer service, checklist confirming the status of the arrival of products and services to the customer.

8.5.5. Post-Delivery activities.

The organization has to ensure that the customer's requirements are met after having delivered the product and service, the responsibility does not end at the time of delivery but must verify the performance of the product and service.

The organization must comply with the guarantees and in some cases the handling of packaging materials, which are considered waste in other words, must comply with all contractual obligations.

8.5.6. Control of changes.

Changes in the production process or service provision have to be documented (description of changes in all stages of the process) and update their standards to avoid the possibility of making mistakes. The changes must be documented according to the established methodology of updating documents.

The organization has to ensure that the changes do not affect the requirements of the products and services.

8.6. Release and products and services.

The products and services have to be released to be sure that all the requirements established with the client are met. This activity must be documented even by the people who authorize this release. These people must be authorized to carry out this activity.

8.7. Control of nonconforming outputs.

8.7.1. Non-conforming outputs (which do not meet the requirements) should not pass to the following processes, much less to the external client, there could be exceptions if the client accepts them but, this must be negotiated and communicated to the relevant interested parties.

Non-conforming outputs can be applied when they are already in the client, these automatically become claims and that is precisely what should be avoided. These non-conforming outputs if they arrive to the client are due in some cases to make a withdrawal of the products.

Non-conforming outputs must be documented to avoid unintentional use. There are organizations that have physical spaces where to place non-conforming outputs and thus ensure they are segregated to avoid possible errors.

Non-conforming outputs can be treated in the following ways:

Correction:	When detecting a non-conforming output, it has to be amended to avoid it. In some cases, if it is allowed, rework and re-process is done.
Separation:	The non-conforming outputs must be separated to avoid their use, they must be correctly identified.
Contention:	If the product has reached the customer, the use of this non-conforming product and service must be contained, and not continue to be used.
Devolution:	If the client does not return it, a product withdrawal must be done.
Suspension of provision of products and services:	Suspend the provisioning of this product and service immediately.
Use under concession:	You can continue with the provisioning of the product and if the client authorizes it by means of an authorization.

8.7.2. The organization will keep documented information of all non-conforming outputs (some organizations handle inventory of non-conforming outputs), of the stages that are generating the non-conformities, of the actions that have been taken, of their effectiveness and of all the resources involved (people, plans, procedures, training, etc.).

9. Performance evaluation.
9.1. Monitoring, measurement, analysis and evaluation.
9.1.1. General.

The organization will determine what it will measure, how it will measure, how it will evaluate the results, what actions it will take, who will measure, what training is necessary, what resources are needed, what are the risks of not measuring or evaluating, where and how will we document the measurement, who and how decisions will be made after the measurement. Si se mide se controla y mejora.

Nowadays organizations do repeatability and reproducibility studies (R & R) of their measurement system:

- Repeatability: How much of the variability in the measurement system is caused by the measuring device.
- Reproducibility: How much of the variability in the measurement system is caused by the differences between the operators.
- If the variability of the measurement system is small compared to the variability of the process.
- If the measurement system is able to distinguish between different parts.
- A good measurement system makes the QMS more reliable.

9.1.2. Customer satisfaction.

The organization has to monitor the perception that the client has about the organization itself and the product and service that is provided. This feedback is essential for the satisfaction of all your requirements.

Regularly to obtain customer satisfaction is done through surveys, physical (reports of visits to customers) or electronic (websites, emails, telephone). It is also valid to use the information of the own evaluations that the clients do of their suppliers, every day this modality is increasing.

Feedback from all clients must be obtained, although if this is not possible, the organization determines in order of importance or criticality of which clients need to obtain feedback. Satisfaction should not only be focused on the external client but also on the internal one.

The organization decides how often to obtain this satisfaction and how it will be obtained. The points to be assessed may vary but should regularly include: The performance of the product and service, the pre-sale and post-sale service, the attention to complaints, the promptness in dealing with complaints and suggestions, the compliance with guarantees, accuracy on dates Agreed, etc.

It also has to establish the degree of satisfaction that is expected to be obtained in the evaluation that is done to the clients.

9.1.3. Analysis and evaluation.

The data obtained from the evaluation by the clients, have to be analyzed by the personnel assigned to the activity and reported to the top management in order to take actions to improve the perception of the clients and focus the whole organization towards the improvement in satisfaction.

It is important that all levels of the organization know what is the perception of the clients and the actions that are being developed to improve or maintain the perception. It is necessary to use statistical techniques and data representation that help the analysis of the data.

The objective is to determine if the QMS is adequate and effective in customer satisfaction.

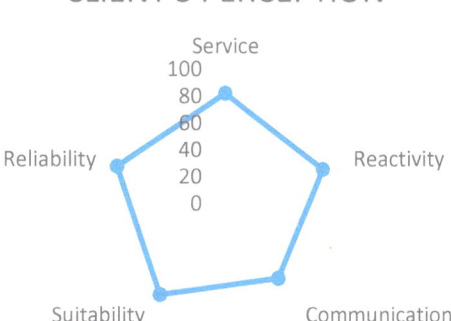

9.2. Internal audit.

9.2.1. Internal audits are an essential tool for the improvement of the QMS, it maintains a continuous monitoring of compliance with what is established as mandatory within the QMS, what is mandatory with the requirements of the standard, legal, customer and those of the organization.

An audit is a random but representative verification process that allows us to establish the efficiency or the veracity of a system, information or procedure. By definition, an internal audit is one that is carried out by people who provide their services to the organization.

The organization must establish a schedule of when the QMS processes will be audited. It is recommended that all processes be audited at least once a year.

The organization must have a team of auditors competent in knowledge of the organization, mastery of the standard, aptitude / attitude to audit, drafting of non-conformities and constant training. It is also increasingly common for organizations to hire external organizations to audit their system, these are called internal audits performed by a second party.

9.2.2. Internal audits have to take into account the following:

Audit programs:	Planning, documentation, follow-up, objectivity and impartiality. Audit program that evaluates the effectiveness of the QMS is to sum up the meeting of all the processes of audit that occur within the organization. When it comes to implementing the frequency of audits, the Organization has to apply risk-based thinking and the importance of processes bone its impact within the system.
Criteria and scope of the audits:	The basis to be applied for the audit, in this case the criterion is ISO 9001: 2015 and the scope is that processes will be audited in the program.
Team of auditors:	Name those who will form the audit team.
Corrective actions	Corrective actions generated by the non-compliances found in the audit.

The results of the audits have to be documented and available for when it is required.

9.3. Management review.
9.3.1. General.

Top management has to review the performance of the QMS and verify if it is aligned with the strategic direction of the organization. The purpose of the review must be to establish whether the QMS is effective, it must be carried out at planned intervals. The revisions can be carried out in a partial way, this means that not all the entries are necessary to be reviewed in a single meeting, but if all of them must be reviewed in an annual period of mandatory form.

9.3.2. Management review inputs.

Information to review in the review by the address:

Status of the actions derived from the previous revision, changes in the external and internal situation of the organization, effectiveness of the QMS, adequacy of resources, risks that affect the organization and opportunities for improvement, any other situation of customers, employees, laws, economic, market aspects that affect the performance of the business.

9.3.3. Management review outputs.

Outputs have to be maintained as documented information.

Management review should be a guide for the performance of the QMS, support it with the resources necessary to improve their effectiveness.

10. Improvement.
10.1. General.

The organization does not have to remain static regarding improving customer satisfaction, taking advantage of all opportunities for improvement, in other words preventing the risks of committing non-conformities and carrying out corrective actions due to deviations in the processes, in order to improve the performance of the QMS and its effectiveness.

The improvement can be made in the QMS, processes and products and services.

10.2. Nonconformity and corrective action.

10.2.1. When a non-conformity is detected, the following activities must be followed:

- Identify the origin of the non-conformity: internal (non-compliant departures, the goal of a quality objective, internal audit, management review, customer satisfaction survey, staff that detects problems, management suggestions), external (customer complaints, suggestions for improvement, certification audits, customer audits, audits by a government entity, warranty claims).

- Identify the corrective action in a unique way to be able to give traceability.

- Assign responsibility for managing non-compliance.

- Carry out immediate correction of non-compliance.

- Carry out an analysis to find the root causes of the problem. Check if this non-conformity is already repeated, that can give a guide. For this analysis you can use the 5 whys and Ishikawa diagram techniques.

- Describe and implement the actions to be followed, place him / her responsible for each action and its end date.

- Review the effectiveness of each of the actions implemented. It will be necessary to ensure that non-compliance does not happen again.

- Update the risk matrix of the processes, verify that these actions that generated the non-compliance are in said matrix.

- Evaluate if the actions taken generated any change in the QMS.

Sample format to record corrective actions

Corrective Action				
Process:	Responsible for the process:	Opening date:		Action Nº:
		Date of follow-up:		
Origin of the action				
Customer satisfaction:		☐	Additional comments	
Customer claims:		☐		
Process trend:		☐		
Measurement of the process:		☐		
Management review:		☐		
Certification audit:		☐		
Surveillance audit:		☐		
Internal audit:		☐		
Customer audit:		☐		
Other:		☐		
Internal audit number:			Internal / External Auditor:	
Description of the non-conformity:		☐	**Description of potential non-conformance:**	☐
Description:			Clause of the norm:	
Description of the immediate action to resolve the non-compliance:				
Root cause analysis:				
1				
2				
Action plan:				
	Activity		In charge of	Date of implementation
1				
2				
Implementation follow-up:				
	Evidence		Date of follow-up	Signature of closing of the action

1			
2			
Revision of efficacy:			
	Evidence	Date of follow-up	Review date
1			
2			

10.2.2. The documented information generated by the implementation of corrective actions must be available and shared with the personnel involved so that all are involved and are aware of the actions that are being taken to avoid non-compliance.

10.3. Continual improvement.

The organization has to continuously improve the suitability, suitability and effectiveness of the QMS. These improvements can document the so-called Improvement Projects.

All the results of the analysis and evaluation have to be considered, in addition to the review by the management. It has to be determined if there are needs and opportunities that have to be considered as part of the continuous improvement.

The organization has to establish the necessary actions to identify the areas of their organization that have low performance and opportunities, in addition to using tools and methodologies necessary to investigate the causes of that low performance and as support to carry out the continuous improvement.

QMS Control knob.

No	Activity	Description	J	F	M	A	M	J	J	A	S	O	N	D
1	Management review	The performance and effectiveness of the entire QMS is reviewed.		10						12				
2	CA Management review	Deadline to submit the CAs.		20						22				

No	Activity	Description	J	F	M	A	M	J	J	A	S	O	N	D
3	Certification Audit	Certification of the system by a certification company.						13						
4	CA Certification audit	If CAs are detected, they must be submitted to the audit for validation						30						
5	Customer satisfaction survey	Conduct customer survey via email.	31											
6	Customer Satisfaction Survey Report	Present to process leaders the results of the satisfaction survey.		7										
7	CA Customer Satisfaction Survey	Processes involved in customer satisfaction should present their CAs.		15										
8	Comprehensive QMS audit	Internal audit of all QMS processes.			2-8						1-7			
9	Report and NC of Integral Audit of the QMS	Date to deliver the CAs due to the audit findings.												
10	Evaluation of performance indicators	Receive and evaluate management indicators according to the goals.	5	5	5	5	5	5	5	5	5	5	5	5
11	AC Evaluation of performance indicators	Maximum date to receive the CAs.	10	10	10	10	10	10	10	10	10	10	10	10
12	AC Tracking	Monitoring of the status of all CAs.	30	28	30	30	30	30	30	30	30	30	30	30
13	Document review	Update procedures, instructions, formats, policies of QMS.										30	30	30

Brief implementation diagram of the QMS.

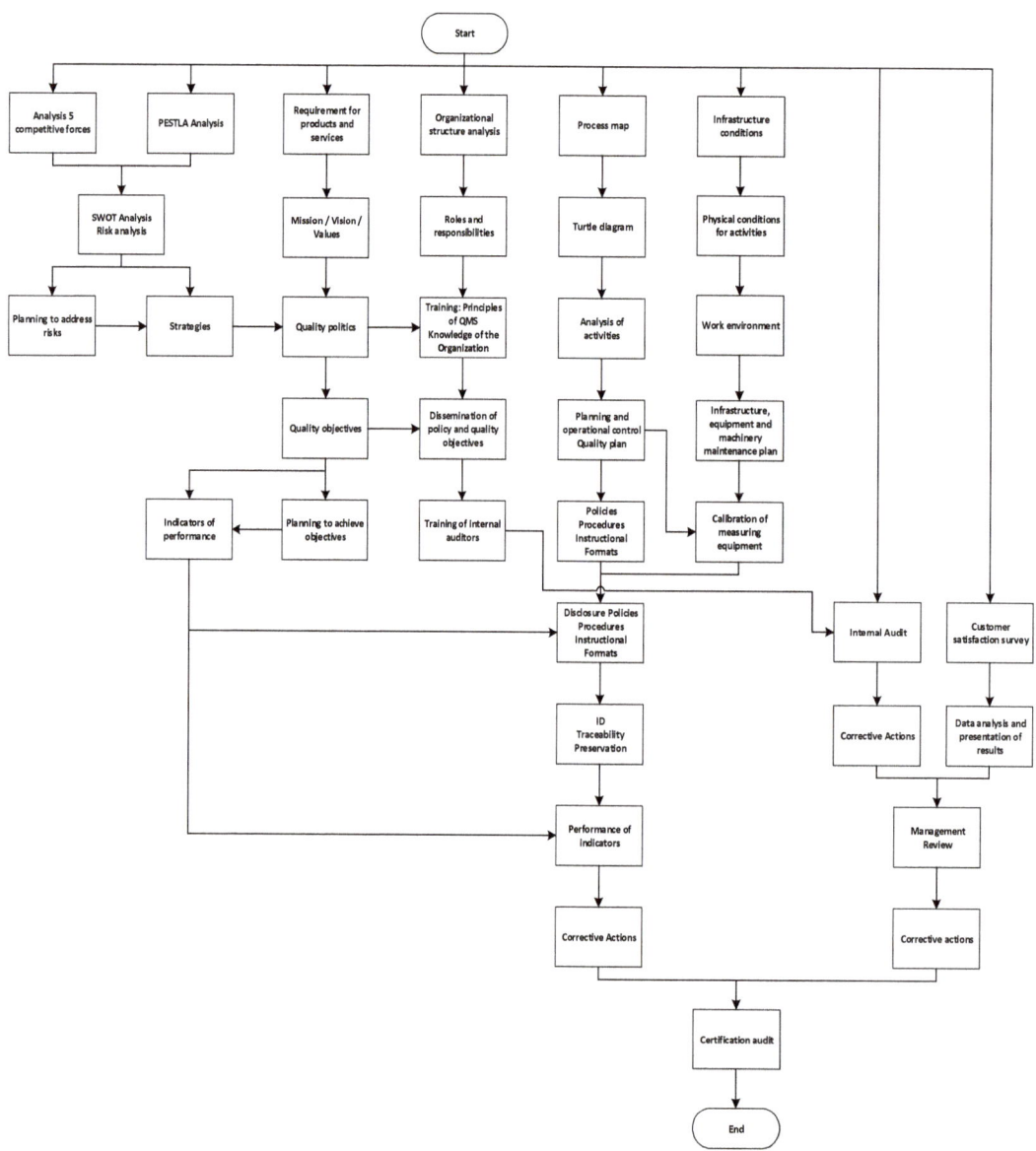

Glossary.

5 Porter competitive forces:	This model establishes a framework to analyze the level of competition within an industry, and to be able to develop a business strategy. This analysis derives in the respective articulation of the 5 forces that determine the intensity of competition and rivalry in an industry, and therefore, in how attractive is this industry in relation to investment opportunities and profitability. These forces are: the possibility of threat before new competitors, the power of the negotiation of the different suppliers, having the capacity to negotiate with the assiduous buyers and the people who will consume it only once, threat of income by secondary products and rivalry among competitors.
Business	Any public, private or non-profit organization.
Context diagram:	Represents a high-level view of an organization, defines the boundaries between the organization and its environment; showing the external stakeholders that interact with the organization and the flow of information that they exchange.
Documented information:	These are procedures, work instructions, visual aids, drawings, specifications, metrics, reports, performance indicators, minutes of meetings, business plan, quality objectives, risks and opportunities, strategies, mission, vision, values and process maps.
Goal:	It is derived from an objective, has the same intention of an objective but is more specific.
Interested Parties:	That person who shows interest in the business of the organization, regardless of whether it has any link with it.
ISO 31000:	Risk Management, Principles and Guidance.
Management Review:	Report of a meeting that must attend Management, the Quality Manager and all that we consider appropriate to review the quality management system and make decisions for the next period based on the results obtained in the cycle that concludes.
Matrix RACI:	Responsible; Accountable; Consulted, Informed.
Matrix RACI-VS:	Verify and Sign roles are assigned.
Matrix RASCI:	Support role is assigned.
Methodology AMFE:	Methodology that is applied when designing new products, services or processes. Its purpose is to study the possible future failures ("failure modes") of our product to later classify them according to their importance.

Methodology COSO:	Methodology capable of addressing risk management in companies from an integrative approach and that means a great opportunity to create value for its stakeholders or stakeholders.
Methodology IRM:	Methodology of the British Institute, are risk management standards that consider the positive and negative consequences in all types of organizations and activities in the short and long term.
Model SIPOCC	SIPOC is the acronym that symbolizes: Suppliers, Entries, Processes, Departures and Clients.
Objective:	It's where you want to go.
PESTLA Analysis:	Analysis of the Political, Economic, Social, Technological, Legal and Environmental environment that positively or negatively affects the organization.
Process:	It is a set of interrelations or interactions of activities that use inputs in order to achieve the expected results.
QMS:	Quality management system.
Strategic:	Actions on how to achieve the objectives.
SWOT Analysis:	An essential tool for the study of the company. The SWOT analysis is a strategic planning tool, designed to perform an internal analysis (Strengths and Weaknesses) and external analysis (Opportunities and Threats) in the company.
Turtle diagram:	The Turtle Diagram is a scheme that contains the elements of a process and adopts the shape of this animal. It has a body, four legs, a head and tail:
	The processes and their transformations are represented in the body. The legs are formed by the key questions that the organization must answer: with what, what are the requirements, how to use the resources, methods to be used. With whom the necessary activities will be done, and finally how those actions will be measured, indicators to be used. The head refers to the input elements of that process in question. The tail is the end, the results that arise from those input elements once they have been processed.

References.

ISO 9000: 2015 Quality Management Systems. Fundamentals and Vocabulary
ISO 9001: 2015 Quality Management Systems - Requirements

Sobre el autor.

CARLOS H HERNANDEZ, Systems Engineer with experience in management of industrial plants and primary plastic packaging for the beverage industry, Post Graduate studies in Business Administration, Risk Prevention and Project Management. Extensive experience in consulting and implementation of management systems based on ISO Standards, as well as Lead Auditor for ISO 9001, 14001, 22000 and OHSAS 18001 standards, as well as university professor and business coach.

Other publications.

- HACCP Concepts & Quick Reference 1era Ed Eng. 2017.

www.ingramcontent.com/pod-product-compliance
Lightning Source LLC
Chambersburg PA
CBHW051213220526
45473CB00003B/1018

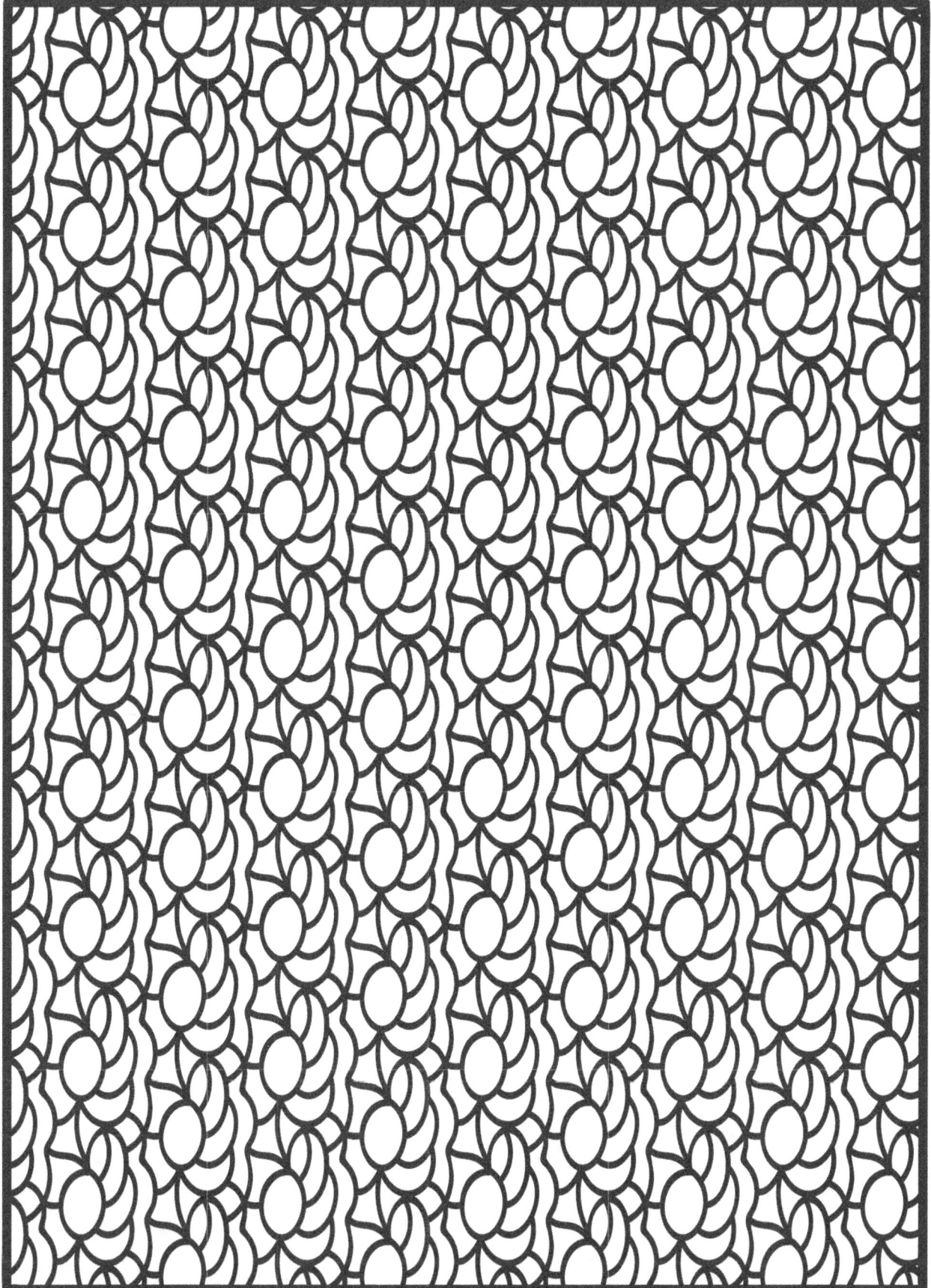

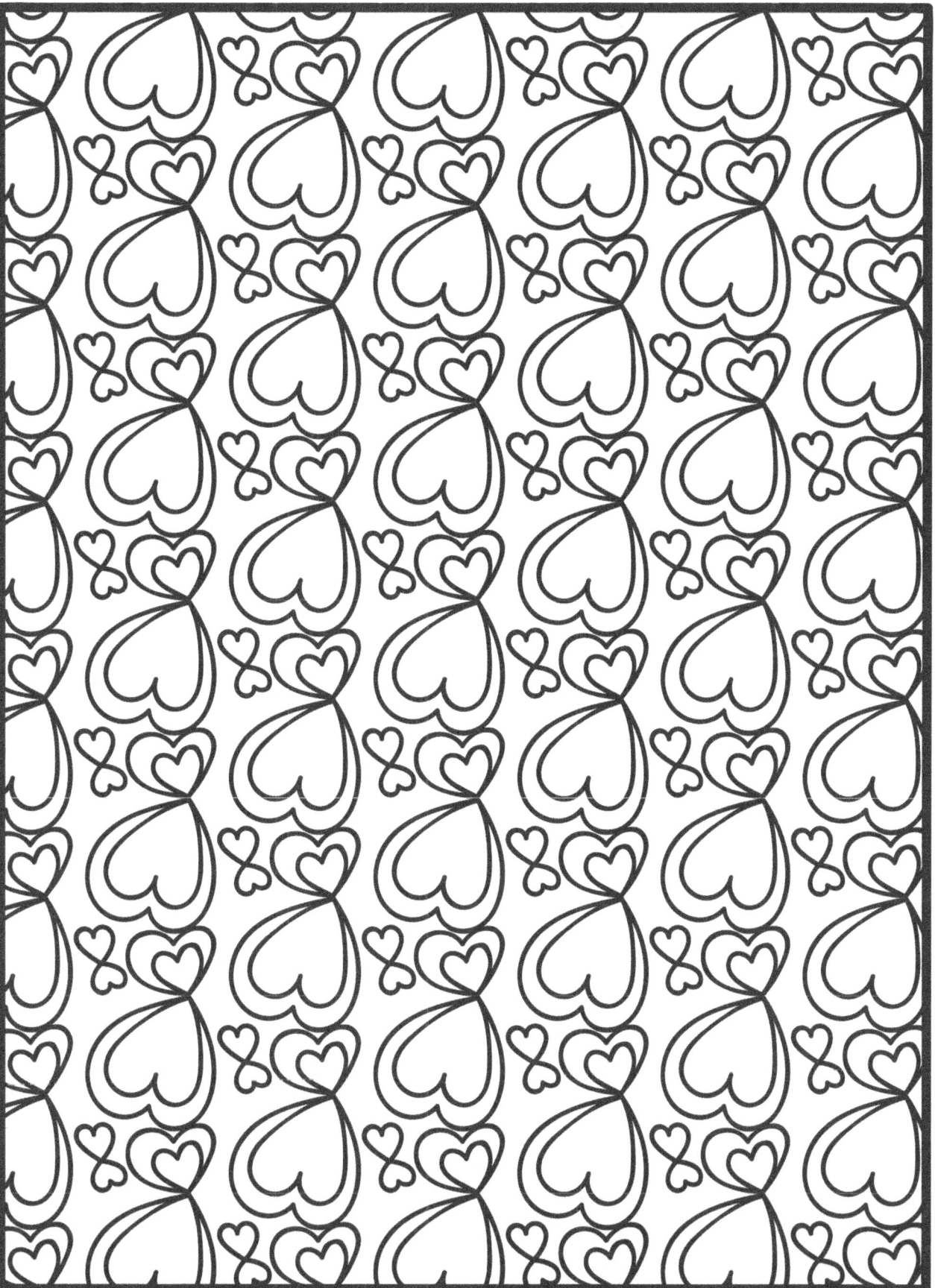

COLOR TEST PAGE

COLOR TEST PAGE

www.ingramcontent.com/pod-product-compliance
Lightning Source LLC
Chambersburg PA
CBHW082119220526
45472CB00009B/2238